S0-AKL-473

SPOTLIGHT ON NATIVE AMERICANS

NEZ PERCE

Topher Royce

PowerKiDS
press.

New York

Published in 2016 by The Rosen Publishing Group, Inc.
29 East 21st Street, New York, NY 10010

First Edition

Editor: Karolena Bielecki
Book Design: Kris Everson
Reviewed by: Robert J. Conley, Former Sequoyah Distinguished Professor at Western Carolina University and Director of Native American Studies at Morningside College and Montana State University
Supplemental material reviewed by: Donald A. Grinde, Jr., Professor of Transnational/American Studies at the State University of New York at Buffalo.

Photo Credits: Cover Marilyn Angel Wynn/Native Stock/Getty Images; pp. 4–5 © Joseph Sohm/Visions of America/age fotostock; pp. 7, 11, 13, 19 Peter Newark's American Pictures; p. 8 North Wind Picture Archives; pp. 10–11 © Guenter Wamser/F1onli/age fotostock; p. 15 Popperfoto/Getty Images; pp. 16, 23, 24, 25 Native Stock; p. 17 Corbis; pp. 20–21 Marilyn Angel Wynn/Nativestock/ Getty Images; p. 27 © Walter Rawlings/Robert Harding Picture Library/ age fotostock; pp. 28–29 American Spirit/Shutterstock.com.

Library of Congress Cataloging-in-Publication Data

Royce, Topher.
 Nez Perce / Topher Royce.
    pages cm. — (Spotlight on Native Americans)
 Includes bibliographical references and index.
 ISBN 978-1-4994-1695-4 (pbk.)
 ISBN 978-1-4994-1696-1 (6 pack)
 ISBN 978-1-4994-1698-5 (library binding)
 1. Nez Percé Indians—History—Juvenile literature. 2. Nez Percé Indians—Social life and customs—Juvenile literature. I. Title.
 E99.N5R69 2016
 979.5004'974124—dc23
                                    2015009050

Manufactured in the United States of America

CPSIA Compliance Information: Batch #WS15PK: For Further Information contact Rosen Publishing, New York, New York at 1-800-237-9932

CONTENTS

ORIGIN OF THE NEZ PERCE

CHAPTER 1

The Nez Perces are a people of Idaho, Washington, and Oregon in the western United States. Today they number about 3,000.

No one knows exactly how the Nez Perce and other Indian tribes got to North America. Like many Native groups, however, the Nez Perces explain their beginnings in an origin story.

According to this story, before there were people in the world, the animals, including Coyote, could talk and act like humans. One day a huge monster called

The Payette River flows through Nez Perce homelands in Idaho.

Iltswewitsix began eating everything in sight. Coyote tied himself to the earth, hoping Iltswewitsix wouldn't eat him up with everything else, but the monster found him. Coyote quickly jumped down Iltswewitsix's throat. He went to the monster's heart, took out his stone knife, and began to cut its body up into pieces. Then he threw the pieces all over the land, creating many different tribes.

When he was done, Coyote realized that no tribe was in the Kamiah Valley in Idaho. Coyote shook some drops of the monster's blood off his fingers and made the last and best tribe, the Nimi'ipuu, or Real People, as the Nez Perces call themselves, right where he stood.

CONTACT WITH EUROPEAN AMERICANS

CHAPTER 2

Sent by President Thomas Jefferson, Meriwether Lewis and William Clark led an **expedition** to map and explore a large part of North America. They met some of the Nez Perce people in 1805. The Nez Perces fed Lewis and Clark's weak and hungry group, helped them make canoes, and guided them toward the Pacific Ocean. In return, Lewis and Clark gave the Nez Perces gifts of cloth, ribbons, and peace medals.

Later meetings with European Americans did not go so well for the Nez Perces. In 1836, a Christian minister, Henry Spalding, and his wife, Eliza, established a **Presbyterian mission** at Lapwai in what is now Idaho. Spalding tried to change the Nez Perces' lifestyle, including their religion. In 1847, some of the Nez Perces told the Spaldings to stop interfering with their way of life, and they attacked the mission, but no one was hurt.

Settlers followed the **missionaries**, bringing their families in covered wagons on the Oregon Trail to live on lands that had been the home of the Nez Perce people, without permission or payment. The settlers also brought diseases, such as smallpox and measles, that killed many Nez Perces between 1846 and 1847.

Many pioneer families packed up their belongings and came west in wagons because they had heard that land was available. Many didn't realize that Native American peoples already lived on the land; some did not care.

THE "THIEF TREATY" AND WAR

CHAPTER 3

Governor Isaac Stevens was placed in charge of the new Northwest Territory, which included Nez Perce lands. He called the Walla Walla **Treaty** Council in 1855, where the Nez Perces agreed to give up much of their

White officials met with Native American chiefs at treaty councils to settle disagreements between the Native Americans and whites.

land in exchange for a 13-million-acre (5 million ha) **reservation** and peace.

Governor Stevens made a new treaty in 1863 that cut the reservation to one-tenth of its size. Chief Joseph and the bands that lived on this land refused to sign the new treaty. However, Governor Stevens convinced other Nez Perce men to sign what is today called the "Thief Treaty."

At first, Chief Joseph and the other bands refused to leave their home. In May 1877, however, General Oliver Otis Howard said that the Nez Perce people must leave or the U.S. Army would come after them. The Nez Perce chiefs finally decided to move to the Lapwai Reservation to avoid war. Three angry young warriors raided a settlement, however, and killed four white men. Realizing this meant war, the Nez Perces fled to White Bird Canyon. The U.S. Army followed the Nez Perces to White Bird Canyon in 1877 and attacked them, but the Nez Perce warriors badly beat the army. The Nez Perce War had begun.

DEATH AT BIG HOLE
CHAPTER 4

After the White Bird Canyon battle, the Nez Perces traveled east over the Bitterroot Mountains and camped at Big Hole, Montana. U.S. troops surprise attacked the camp and killed many Nez Perces, mostly women and children. The Nez Perces continued running, this time north toward Canada, knowing the army couldn't cross the Canadian border. General Howard asked Colonel Nelson Miles to take his troops ahead of the fleeing Nez Perces and cut them off in northern Montana.

The tired and hungry Nez Perces made camp only 40 miles (64 km) from the Canadian border. General Miles's troops reached them and attacked. The Nez Perces agreed to surrender if they could return to the Lapwai Reservation in Idaho.

Despite the agreement with General Miles, other army generals ignored these terms and sent 431 Nez Perces to Fort Leavenworth, Kansas. In 1878, after much illness and death, they were moved to Indian Territory in present-day Oklahoma.

In 1885, exile finally ended. Although 431 Nez Perces surrendered in 1877, only 268 left Oklahoma in 1885. Some returned to Lapwai, but Chief Joseph and his warriors were sent to the Colville reservation in present-day Washington State, where their **descendants** still live today.

At his surrender, Chief Joseph said, "Hear me, my chiefs, I am tired. My heart is sick and sad. From where the sun now stands, I will fight no more forever."

Big Hole Valley, Montana

TRADITIONAL CYCLES OF LIFE

CHAPTER 5

Before the mid-1800s, the Nez Perces lived in small bands and moved each season to find food. In spring, the Nez Perces caught salmon. They ate some of the fish and dried the rest to preserve it for winter. The Nez Perces hunted elk, moose, deer, rabbit, squirrel, duck, and grouse year-round.

In summer, the Nez Perces would travel to the mountains. The women gathered roots, greens, and berries. Camas root (lily bulbs) was the most important food, but bitterroot, couse (biscuitroot), wild onions, wild carrots, huckleberries, and chokecherries were all gathered.

The permanent winter home of the Nez Perce people was the longhouse, which could be more than 100 feet (30 m) long and shelter many families. An **A-frame** constructed over a long oblong hole supported the roof and walls, which were hung with woven mats. Most Nez Perce bands used tepees for temporary homes when traveling (an idea borrowed from the Plains Indians).

The Nez Perce people began to use the tepee after trading with the Plains Indians. Made with wooden poles, the tepee was covered by **tule** mats, bison skins, or later on, canvas.

Clothing was made from animal hides. Fringes, beads, quills, paint, and other things, like elk teeth, often decorated the shirts and leggings worn by the men and the loose dresses worn by the women. Both men and women wore moccasins made from hides.

NEZ PERCE LEADERSHIP
CHAPTER 6

Small bands of Nez Perce people gathered in villages near streams where fish and water were available. Villages contained several families and were led by a headman, usually the oldest active man. While the headman was a spokesman for the village and solved disagreements, the village council, which included the male heads of all of the families, made most of the decisions that affected each village. Since the Nez Perces were made up of many different bands, they didn't really have a chief for the whole tribe.

The Nez Perce leaders were powerful because they could convince people to respect and follow them. They did not give orders but rather led by example and **persuasion**. If they were fair, honest, and generous and their lives provided a good model for the young to follow, people admired them.

Usually the headmen were peace chiefs, known for their wisdom, concern for people, and **eloquent** speech. However, other village leaders were war chiefs—brave, experienced warriors who led the men in battle. Sometimes the headmen were **medicine men**.

Nez Perce headmen were often chosen because their fathers were also chiefs or because they were highly respected.

GROWING UP NEZ PERCE

CHAPTER 7

Babies were born in a small, separate "women's house." The mother was helped during birth by her own mother and other women. Young children spent most of their time with their grandparents, who taught them basic household tasks and told them stories. At about age three, they also began to participate in

The Nez Perce people still teach their children the "old ways." Here, the children's first kill and first root gathering are celebrated.

food-gathering activities, helping their relatives hunt, fish, dig for roots, or gather berries.

When boys became teenagers, they were often sent out alone to seek **visions** and find their helping spirit, or *wyakin*. Girls could undertake a vision quest, too, but they also had a special ceremony when they became adults at about age twelve or thirteen. They stayed alone in a hut for a week until they were

After birth, babies were bound into **cradleboards** so they could be carried until they began to walk.

welcomed back to the village with gifts to take their place as women ready for marriage.

Families often arranged marriages. If both families felt that the match were a good one, the young people began living together. After a ceremony and gift exchange was completed, the young people were officially married.

TRADITIONAL BELIEFS

CHAPTER 8

The Nez Perces believed that all living things had spirits. They tried to live in harmony with the mountains, trees, rivers, and animals and respect their spirits. Through dreams and visions, people received power from spirits and communicated with them. Having **supernatural** power was important to the Nez Perce way of life. Young people went on vision quests to discover their spirit helper and to explore how its supernatural power could be helpful.

The people who gained the most power from their spirit helpers were the tribe's medicine men and women. They could cure sick people, affect the weather, or predict the future of a hunting or war party. They also helped others find their spirit helpers and were in charge of the tribe's dances and ceremonies.

The Nez Perces who followed these traditional beliefs were known as "Dreamers." Often, the Dreamers and the Christian Nez Perces disagreed on matters. Many Dreamers didn't sign the Thief Treaty in 1863 and fought

Jason, a Nez Perce medicine man. Nineteenth-century medicine men and women were important and respected in Nez Perce society.

in the Nez Perce War, while the Christian Nez Perces became the "treaty Indians" who lived on the Lapwai Reservation. Today, the Seven Drums Religion of the Nez Perce people recognizes and follows the traditional beliefs of the Dreamers.

CONTEMPORARY NEZ PERCE

CHAPTER 9

The old Lapwai Reservation in Idaho, which today is known as the Nez Perce Nation, covers about 750,000 acres (303,644 ha) in north-central Idaho. The tribe provides jobs and also works to make Nez Perce **culture** and language available to the young people. The Nez Perce Tribal Executive Committee, an elected nine-person committee, governs the reservation's tribal affairs.

The tribe farms over 37,000 acres (15,000 ha) of land. Wheat is the main crop. As well as harvesting timber and mining limestone on the reservation, the tribe owns a chain of grocery stores. **Casinos** near Lewiston and Kamiah on the reservation have provided the tribe with funds and are popular with tourists.

Descendants of Chief Joseph, Yellow Wolf, Yellow Bull, and the other captured warriors still live on the Colville Reservation in Washington State. These Nez Perces are part of the Colville Confederated Tribes community. The Colville Confederated Tribes consist of the Colville, Nespelem, San Poil, Lake, Palus, Wenatchi, Chelan, Entiat, Methow, Southern Okanogan, Moses Columbia, and Nez Perces of Chief Joseph's band. Together, they serve on the tribal council and work for the good of the entire reservation.

Horseback riders in traditional dress take the Nez Perce Trail to a memorial at Bear Paw Battlefield, Montana.

IMPORTANT ISSUES

CHAPTER 10

Today, although a large number of students don't graduate, many young Nez Perces see a good education as important for gaining employment later. Some adult Nez Perce who feel they missed out on education at school are now taking part in distance learning courses in Lapwai and Kamiah. Courses are provided by more distant colleges such as Lewis-Clark State College in Lewiston, Idaho, and the Northwest Indian College in Bellingham, Washington. If they graduate, these adults usually go on to four-year college courses.

Nez Perce children are encouraged to learn about their history by visiting their historic sites. Preserving the language, however, is much more difficult, even though it is taught in schools. Only about twenty fluent Nez Perce speakers are left.

The Nez Perce tribal government runs many health campaigns, such as disease prevention and weight management. It also produces newsletters and posters on health issues. Now the Nez Perces are becoming

There are three thousand members of the Nez Perce tribe today. Of these, sixteen hundred live on the reservation.

more aware of what causes common health problems, such as diabetes and heart disease, and what they can do to improve their health. The tribe recently built the Nimiipuu Health Center in Lapwai, which includes a fitness room with up-to-date exercise equipment.

POWWOWS

CHAPTER 11

The Nez Perce tribe sponsors a number of annual **powwows**, dances, and memorials that feature music, drumming, dancing, crafts, and food. During the first weekend in March at Lapwai, the E-Peh-Tas Powwow features competitive war dancing, while the Mata'Lyma Powwow and Root Feast is held in Kamiah during the third weekend of May with traditional dancing. The Warriors Memorial Powwow during the third weekend of June honors Chief Joseph and his warriors. In August, the Nez Perce War Memorial (Big Hole) is held, and the Bears Paw War Memorial is in October.

At the Nez Perce Tamaliks Wallowa Band powwow in Oregon, people wear traditional clothing, eat traditional foods, and perform traditional dances.

During a powwow, tribal members and guests come together to celebrate Nez Perce history and tradition. The Nez Perce people like to share their culture and teach others about it.

Until 120 years ago, the Nez Perce tribe had occupied the Wallowa Valley, a remote area in northeastern Oregon, for thousands of years. Then the U.S. government took away their traditional homelands. In June 1997, however, the Nez Perces took ownership of 10,300 acres (4,170 ha) of former cattle-ranching land in Wallowa. Currently a wildlife habitat, the land is now used for Nez Perce cultural and spiritual events and powwows.

ART AND LITERATURE
CHAPTER 12

Thanks to Archie Phinney (1903–1949), much of the Nez Perce language and many of its stories have been preserved for future generations. Phinney was born on the reservation and raised as a native speaker in a traditional manner. After studies at the University of Kansas and Columbia University, he returned to the reservation and wrote books and essays, including a collection of traditional tribal stories. Elizabeth Wilson (1882–1973), a relative of Chief Joseph, also recorded many Nez Perce traditional stories.

There are several Nez Perce authors writing today. Dr. William S. Penn (1949–) has written many books, including books of essays and short stories, as well as novels. In 1994, he won the North American Indian Prose Award. In one of his novels, *Killing Time with Strangers,* one of the characters is a *wyakin,* or spirit helper. Joe McLellan (1945–), a teacher, has written a series of children's books. The books are about a boy and a girl (Billy and Nonie), but the main character is their teacher, Nanabosho, who is part spirit and part person.

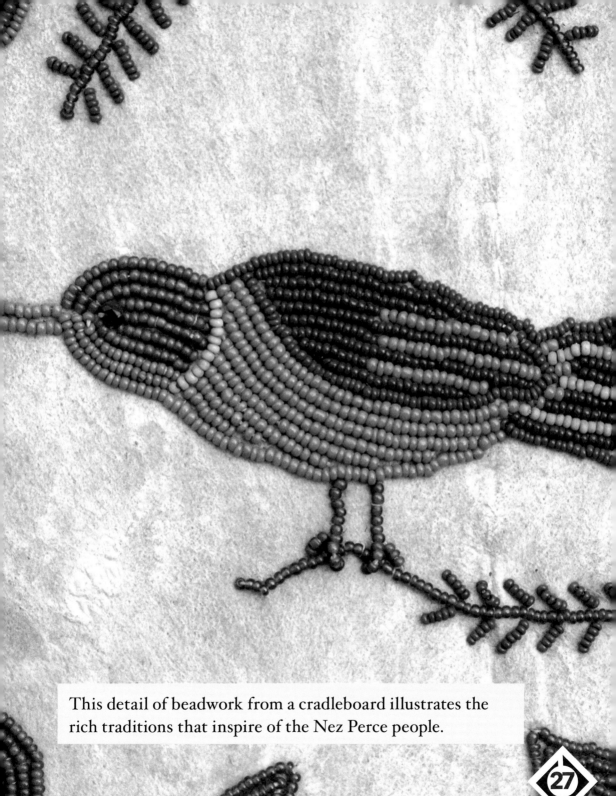

This detail of beadwork from a cradleboard illustrates the rich traditions that inspire of the Nez Perce people.

PRESERVATION

CHAPTER 13

For centuries, one of the most important natural resources for the Nez Perces has been the fish in the Columbia River system. Today, the Nez Perce tribal fisheries department employs more than two hundred people. In recent years, the Nez Perce people have gone to court to protect their fishing rights so they can continue to fish in this area and use traditional net fishing methods. They have established the right to hunt, fish, and gather on 10,000 acres (4,000 ha) of their traditional lands, some of which are not tribally owned. In 1977, the Nez

Perces joined with the Yakima, Warmsprings, and Umatilla tribes to form the Columbia River Inter-Tribal Fisheries Commission. In the 1990s, the commission developed projects to restore the salmon and steelhead trout runs in the Columbia River Basin. These species of fish have declined because of loss of habitat, poor water quality, and overfishing.

The Nez Perces today are a strong and growing Native American nation. They use traditional strengths to build a community that works in the modern world. By looking both to the past and the future, the Nez Perce people will survive as a nation.

Every year, many thousands of salmon migrate from the Pacific Ocean back to the Clearwater River system to breed. Today, the Nez Perces are helping the salmon survive and flourish.

GLOSSARY

A-frame: A support structure shaped like the letter A.

casino: A building where gambling takes place.

cradleboard: Portable cradles made of a board or frame onto which a baby is secured with blankets or binding.

culture: The arts, beliefs, and customs that form a people's way of life.

descendant: Proceeding from people who lived long before you.

eloquent: Having or showing the ability to use language clearly and effectively.

expedition: A trip made for a certain purpose.

medicine man: A religious leader and healer.

mission: A church or group of buildings where people of one religion try to teach people of another religion their beliefs.

missionary: A person who tries to teach others their religion.

persuasion: The act of causing people to do or believe something.

powwow: A social gathering of Native Americans that usually includes dancing.

Presbyterian: Of or relating to a kind of Protestant Christian church.

reservation: Land set aside by the government for specific Native American tribes to live on.

supernatural: Unable to be explained by science or the laws of nature.

treaty: An agreement among nations or people.

tule: A type of plant that grows in swampy lowlands.

vision: Something that you see or dream, especially as part of a supernatural experience.

FOR MORE INFORMATION

BOOKS

Gibson, Karen Bush. *Native American History of Kids: With 21 Activities.* Chicago, IL: Chicago Review Press, 2010.

Schwartz, Heather E. *Seeking Freedom: Causes and Effects of the Flight of the Nez Perce.* Mankato, MN: Capstone Press, 2015.

Tieck, Sarah. *Nez Perce.* Edina, MN: ABDO, 2015.

WEBSITES

Due to the changing nature of Internet links, PowerKids Press has developed an online list of websites related to the subject of this book. This site is updated regularly. Please use this link to access the list: www.powerkidslinks.com/sona/nez

INDEX